BILLY CASPER'S
GOLF TIPS

Edited by Byron Casper

This edition published by Pastime Publications Ltd,
5/9 Rennie's Isle, Edinburgh EH6 6QA.
Tel/Fax: +44 (0) 131 553 4444
E-mail: pastime@btconnect.com

Edited by Byron Casper

2002 © Pastime Publications Ltd.
No part of Billy Casper's Golf Tips may be published or reproduced in any form without the prior consent of the publisher

Pastime Publications are proud to have been accepted as members of Scotland the Brand, an organisation committed to promoting the excellence of Scottish products, services and facilities throughout Scotland and the World. The distinctive blue and red tartan Scotland mark signifies outstanding quality.

Design by ALMOND www.almondtds.com
UK and Worldwide distribution

Contents

4	Introduction by Byron Casper
10	Introduction by Billy Casper
11	Billy Casper - Personal Bio
12	Billy Casper - Golf Legend
18	Introduction
21	The Grip
25	The Stance
31	The Swing
45	Fairway Shots
65	Around the Green
79	On the Green
90	Interview with Billy Casper

Introduction - Byron Casper

Billy Casper is a man who beat the odds to become one of America's top professional golfers. From an early age growing up in New Mexico and California, he learned the hard way how to stand on his own two feet. He started learning the game of golf at age 4, from his Father and Grandfather, eventually playing competitively in junior programs and then High School. During this time he also caddied at the San Diego Country Club for pocket money. After High School he was offered a golf scholarship to Notre Dame University, but only lasted one year in the Indiana cold before packing up his clubs and returning to San Diego.

Having grown up on the streets from the age of 12, Billy's choices were limited and he turned to the Navy for the security he sought in his life. It was during this time in service that he married his long-term girlfriend, Shirley, and began to earn a reputation for both his game and his teaching ability. Billy's talents did not go unnoticed in the Navy and a benevolent Admiral, recognizing his potential, effected an introduction that led to a sponsorship deal. And so, in 1955, Billy Casper made his first professional assault on the PGA tour. His first check ever was for $33.33 in the Western Open 1955.

A lot has happened in the last 48 years. There are very few awards or honors that have avoided a place in the Casper trophy cabinet. Billy's particular reputation as a master of the short game and king of the greens is legendary around the golf world.

Introduction - Byron Casper

In his personal life, he has 11 children, has fostered another 5, and now has 21 grandchildren and 2 great-grandchildren! Not just a great and talented golfer, but a great father too, I'm proud to say that Billy Casper is also my Dad.

And let me tell you, growing up the child of a celebrity leaves you with some unique memories. It seemed slightly strange to me that this man, who I thought was just a pretty normal Dad, kept being besieged for autographs and appearances everywhere we went.

I remember going to restaurants with my father and having people come up for autographs and pictures, or even just to shake his hand.

I remember when I was about 10 years old, in third or fourth grade, one day we were all ushered into the school hall to watch a Disney film called "The Invisible Man". About halfway through the film, two professional golfers appeared – and one of them was Dad! I actually ended up pretty embarrassed by all the attention that brought me at school.

I remember when he captained the US Ryder Cup team and the pride he had in his team and his ability as their Captain.

But I also remember the times when, after long travel schedules and tournaments, he came home and

Introduction - Byron Casper

wanted nothing more than to just spend time with the family and maybe play his favorite video game: Ms. Pac Man! It was unique growing up in this atmosphere because when Dad was home from work, he really was just "Dad"!

Another of my earliest memories is of the Billy Casper golf camp, which I got to attend every year religiously from the age of 8. This was a junior golf camp in California that ran throughout the summer months and catered to junior golfers worldwide.

It was a fantastic experience - I got to meet and compete with other juniors from around the world for three weeks every summer. What I really remember about those summers though, is the one on one time Dad gave to each and every single junior. He was always a great teacher and he had a tremendous amount of patience with the students he worked with.

Over the last 15 years, I have made the transformation from son to business colleague and now editor/publisher, and I have learned a lot about Dad in that time. The one thing that always comes back to impress me though, time and again, is the dedication, skill and love that my Father has for the game of golf. Let's face it, the game we all love so much gives us grief at the worst of times and joy when we are playing well: it is a difficult game with a very small margin for error. It is these tiny margins that make or break the professionals in any sport. But in golf, you are on your own out on the course with nobody else to rely on and it is that aspect which, in my opinion, makes it more nerve-wracking and emotional than any other.

Introduction - Byron Casper

This golf tips book is an accumulation of Billy's best tips and short lessons, which will help you not only to score better, but also to learn or re-learn a few of the fundamentals, which are sometimes lost on middle to high handicappers. This book talks a lot about "Playing within yourself" and "Playing your own game", both of which are paramount to we low handicap golfers in particular, as well as to anyone striving to become a better golfer, which, let's be honest, we all are!

I'm sure you'll enjoy reading and using Billy Casper's Golf Tips as much as I enjoyed working with Dad in putting it together. It is an honor for me to be involved in this book as a son and also as a golfer who has spent a large amount of time teaching and playing the game of golf.

I can vouch for the lessons in this book personally: I learned them first hand - and now you can benefit from them too.

Good luck, enjoy reading and as Dad always says, "Keep your head down...and...follow through!"

Introduction - Billy Casper

Golf has been my life from an early age and I feel very fortunate to have attained so many of my goals. I have a tremendous amount of respect and love for the game of golf and through my new golf tips book, I hope to do two things: Make the basic fundamentals of golf easy to follow and fun to learn, and tap into my 50 years as a professional, giving you a few insights into the life the game of golf has given me.

Your local professional can help you improve your game and that is exactly why they are there, to help you learn and give advice on equipment. My golf tips book can help to give you the edge out on the course and can work nicely in sync with your local professional's knowledge.

I enjoyed putting this together with my son, Byron. I hope you enjoy reading it and using it as a guide to your golf swing and game.

Have a great round!

Billy Casper - Personal Bio

Birthdate: June 24, 1931

Birthplace: San Diego, CA

College: Notre Dame

Joined PGA Tour: 1955

Joined Senior PGA Tour: 1981

Residence: Chula Vista, CA

Family: Wife, Shirley Franklin; Children: Linda, Billy, Robert, Byron, twins Judi and Jeni, Charles, David, Julia, Sarah, Tommy; 21 grandchildren; 2 great grandchildren

Miscellaneous: Very active now with his affiliated companies in Golf Course Design, Golf Course Management, Nutrition, Golf Tours and Teaching. Lists Ben Hogan, Byron Nelson and Sam Snead as his heroes. Has been heavily involved in the annual King Hassan II Trophy tournament in Morocco. Takes an active part in his church.

Billy Casper - Golf Legend

During his professional career, Billy Casper has won national titles on three continents and is credited with more than 70 professional tournament championships, 51 of which were won on the PGA Tour. Among the many titles he has won are the U.S. Open (1959 & 1966); The Masters (1970); and the Canadian Open (1967).

In addition, Billy Casper was elected PGA Player of the Year in 1966 and 1970; selected eight times as a member of the United States Ryder Cup Team; and chosen as the non-playing Ryder Cup Team captain in 1979. He was also a five-time Vardon Trophy winner, an honor awarded each year to the professional golfer with the lowest scoring average on the PGA tour. He was also the second player in the history of the game to surpass the 1 million-dollar mark in prize money alone and the first to surpass $200,000 in a single season. In recognition of his illustrious playing career, Billy Casper was inducted into the World Golf Hall of Fame in 1978 and the PGA Hall of Fame in 1982. Billy Casper has also won eleven titles on the Senior PGA Tour.

Billy Casper - Golf Legend

51 PGA TOUR WINS, INCLUDING
- Tour Championships
- Labatt Open, 1956
- Phoenix Open, 1957
- Kentucky Derby Open, 1957
- Bing Crosby Championship, 1958
- Buick Open, 1958
- U.S. Open, Mamaroneck, NY, 1959
- Western Open, 1965, 1966 & 1973
- U.S. Open, San Francisco, CA 1966
- Canadian Open, 1967
- Masters, 1970
- Los Angeles Open, 1970
- Kaiser International Open, 1971
- Sammy Davis Jr./Greater Hartford Open, 1973
- New Orleans Open, 1975

11 SENIOR PGA WINS
- Senior Tour Championships
- Shootout at Jeremy Ranch, 1982
- Merrill Lynch/
  Golf Digest Commemorative Pro-Am, 1982
- USGA Senior Open, 1983
- Legends of Golf, 1984
- Senior PGA, 1984
- Greater Grand Rapids Open, 1987
- Del Webb Arizona Classic, 1987
- Vantage Tournament, 1988
- Mazda Senior TPC, 1988
- Japan Urbanet Championship, 1989
- Transamerica Open, 1989

Billy Casper – Golf Legend

ADDITIONAL ACHIEVEMENTS
- Sixth on PGA Tour's All-Time Victories list
- Play off record on the PGA Tour: Played 8, Won 8
- Ryder Cup Team, 1961, 1963, 1965, 1967, 1969, 1971, 1973, 1975 and Captain 1979
- Two-time PGA Player of the Year, 1966 & 1970
- Five-time Vardon Trophy Winner, 1960, 1963, 1965, 1966 & 1968
- Inducted in World Golf Hall of Fame, 1978
- Inducted in PGA Hall of Fame, 1982
- Over 10 International wins including: Brazilian Open, 1959, 1960; Italian Open, 1975; Mexican Open, 1977

PERSONAL

Named Golfweek's Father of the Year for 1996 and was selected as the Memorial Tournament's honoree that same season. Received the Jimmy Demaret Award at the 1996 Liberty Mutual Legends of Golf. Was also the honoree at the 1997 Nissan Open in Los Angeles. In 2001 he was honored by the Moroccan Royal family with the equivalent of a knighthood.

Introduction

Golf is the greatest game in the world. It is frustrating, humiliating, humbling and exciting. It can get you down and make you scream and it can give you satisfaction and joy. Golf teaches us about life and ourselves; putting our characters to the test; requiring patience, restraint and skill.

I first started to understand this on June 16, 1966. It was the first time I learned the value of restraint. All sorts of thoughts were going through my head on the sixteenth hole at the Olympic Club in San Francisco during the US Open Championship. Only a few holes before, I had been a hopelessly beaten man. Paired with Arnold Palmer as the tournament's leading twosome, I had fallen seven shots back with only nine holes left to play. My only hope at this stage appeared to be avoiding complete disgrace. Suddenly, the match took an unbelievable turn.

I snaked in a putt on the 13th, then on the 15th I birdied and Palmer bogeyed. Suddenly, I was only 3 shots back and for the first time I felt that I had a chance to win. On the 16th (604 yard, par 5, dog leg left) I teed the ball up and looked down the narrow canyon of the fairway with large trees lining it and an inner voice said to me "Go for it! This is no time to be chicken". Tension gripped me and I was so shaken that I stepped away from the ball. I said to myself, "Just play your game, play within yourself." I took a nice easy swing and the ball sailed through the air right down the middle.

Palmer teed up and his drive struck a tree 180 yards down the fairway. Arnold has always been a great competitor and he has thrilled crowds with the way he attacks a golf course and swings a club. He grabbed a 3 iron and tried to get the ball back in position, but

Introduction

found himself hitting his 5th shot from a bunker close to the green. On the other hand, I played a nice easy 2nd shot and then a nice mid iron 13 feet from the hole. Arnold got down in two from the bunker for a six and I sank my putt for a birdie 4 putting me only one shot behind. We subsequently tied for the title and the next day went into an 18 hole playoff. Arnold came in with a 73 and I won the tournament with a 69. I often wonder what the result might have been if I had given in to my first impulse and tried to go for it.

My first advice for anyone wishing to play golf is to both enjoy it and play your own game. The professionals at your local course are there to help you find your game and can be of great help. Do not try to kill the ball. Relax. Swing easy and learn to play safe and score. It was the great Bobby Jones who said, "Golf is a game played on a five inch course – the distance between the ears". Ben Hogan expressed the same philosophy in a more direct fashion. He said, "Golf is 30% physical and 70% mental". Golf is different from a lot of mainstream sports. In other sports, there is a certain amount of automatic reflex because of the moving ball.

Introduction

In golf, you are hitting a stationary ball toward a fixed target, which brings a much more mental aspect to the game. But the brain cannot process too much information at the same time and so it stands to reason that if you are about to hit a shot and you're thinking: "My hands need to be here and my wrists should be cocked at the top and I should swing easy and keep my eyes on the ball", etc. this endless list can crack up your game. The goal of a tournament golfer, and any golfer for that matter, is to cultivate a swing that you can repeat over and over again, without having to think too much about it. You should be thinking about the playability of your shots and the course and not get lost on the swing itself!

The main purpose of this book is to outline the basic fundamentals of golf and some of the various shots you might find yourself taking on the course. I have won a lot of events and made a considerable amount of money doing it but a good golf swing for me is not necessarily for you, so please use this book and learn from the tips, tricks and shots outlined but use your own particular style: the style that makes you hit the ball the same way over and over again. Remember you have only one brain and over a thousand muscles! Don't think too much, and learn to hit all the clubs in your bag. There is a reason why you're allowed 14 clubs, so use them all.

After the basics of stance, grip and swing I like to focus on what I call the 3 T's. These are tempo, touch and thinking. Collectively we might call them concentration. It is so important to concentrate on what you are doing without getting down about missed or bad shots. Forgive yourself and play the next shot.

THE GRIP

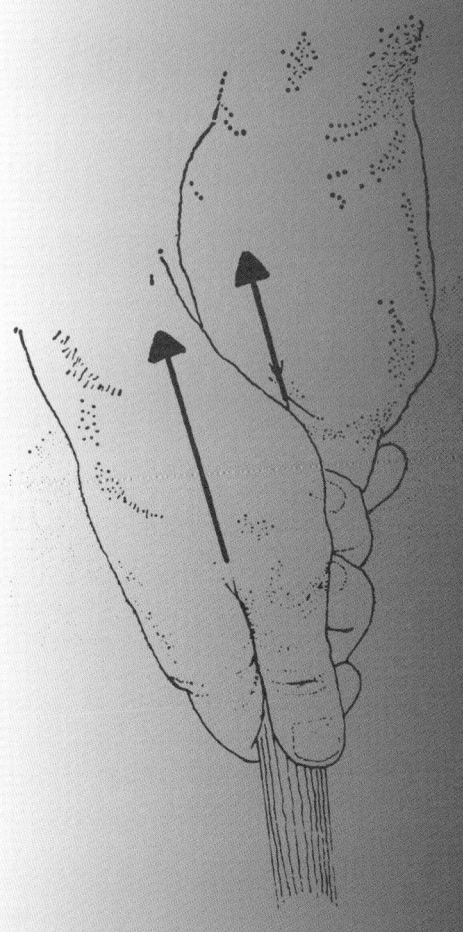

The Grip

The grip is the most important fundamental of golf. Only about 1 in 100 golfers use a proper grip, yet it is the only contact a player has with the ball. The hands make contact with the club and then the ball. You could say the grip is the outlet or gearbox for the body's power through the golf shot. If it is faulty, it makes it even harder for you to hit the ball the way you want to. Whereas a swing can be individual to a player, the grip will remain the same in one of three ways. Harry Vardon, the inventor of the modern golf grip, had a terrible time with calluses on the palms of his hands from the rough oak tree branches they shaped into golf clubs back on his native Jersey around the turn of the century. It was this problem that caused him to invent the light finger grip or the overlapping grip. The variations of this group are the interlocking grip where the fingers are locked together and the baseball grip where the fingers are all on the grip and not overlapping at all. Harry Vardon won 6 British Open Championships between 1896 and 1914 and became a model for style and incredible skill on the island where golf was invented. Vardon always disliked the term "grip", he preferred "gently hold" or "caress" the club in the hands.

Deciding how to take a grip can be confusing to the higher handicap golfer and junior. There is an easy way to show the relationship between the grip and the club's face, which can be helpful.

The Grip

Make it a point to align the palm of your left hand with the clubface lining up the club at what you're aiming at. When this is done you will have the best chance of a solid hit with the face of the club on line with your target. All you have to do then is make sure the back of your left hand swings towards your target at and after impact with the ball.

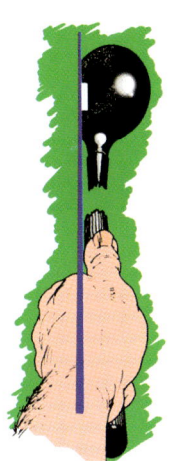

To play your best, take a grip that allows your wrists to hinge as you swing. The best grip uses more fingers than the palm. The left hand controls positioning and is placed on the club first. The club runs diagonally across the middle of the forefinger. When the hand is folded over the club, the thumb should be slightly right of centre with the last three fingers gripping firmly. The "V" formed by the thumb and forefinger should point roughly towards the right shoulder.

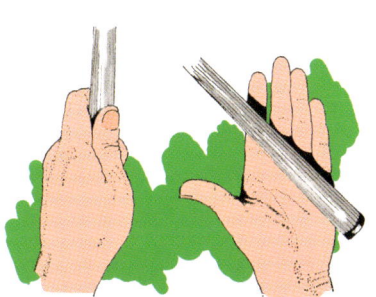

The Grip

The right hand grip should be in the fingers for the most effective feel and sensitivity. When the right hand is opened, you should see the club run from the junction of the little finger across the middle of the forefinger. In the popular Vardon overlap grip, the right little finger curls over the left forefinger. In the interlock grip the right little finger locks between the left forefinger and middle finger and in the baseball grip the right little finger grips the club next to the left forefinger.

While your grip on the club should never be rigid and intense, there are some pressure points all golfers should know.

Since the left hand is placed on the club first, let's start there. The most pressure should be felt in the last three fingers. This firmness should be particularly felt at the top of the backswing. If they loosen at this point, your control will be lost.

In the right hand, firmness should be felt in the thumb and forefinger, not so much when you're addressing the ball or even during your backswing but at the impact point. If your right hand loosens here the clubface can move out of the "square position" and the ball will go offline.

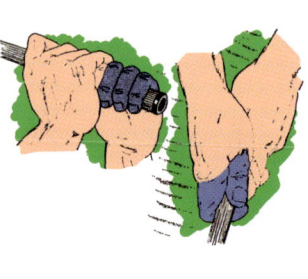

THE STANCE

The Stance

The stance is basically standard among most top golfers. The right foot is at a right angle to the line of the ball flight. The left foot is pointed slightly left. Some tournament players like to have the toes of both feet pointed outwards, but I have never felt that the actual position of the toes makes much difference except for comfort.

The stance provides balance. It determines direction and gives power. Once you learn the proper stance you should try to make it instinctive and as natural as walking up to the ball.

There are some basic rules on the width of the stance. It varies with the type of club being used. The stance is wider with woods and long irons and much more narrow when using short irons and lofted clubs. On medium irons, my personal tendency has always been to have my stance approximately shoulder width and then I am able to make it wider or more narrow depending upon the shot. A tendency to be avoided is taking too wide a stance with your driver. This can cause the hips to swing and not only will you lose power you will lose control too. A stance that is comfortable to your game and one that can be copied over and over again is what you should be looking for.

The Stance

There are 3 basic stances in golf depending on what result you want. For most players the square stance is best for full shots and longer clubs. In this stance, the feet are equal distance apart and the toes are lined up to the line of flight of the ball. This will most likely produce a straight shot.

The open stance has the left foot slightly withdrawn towards the body and pointed a little left. This will produce a "fade" or "slice" causing the ball to move from left to right.

The closed stance has the right foot slightly withdrawn towards the body and pointed a little right. This will produce a "draw" or "hook" causing the ball to move from right to left.

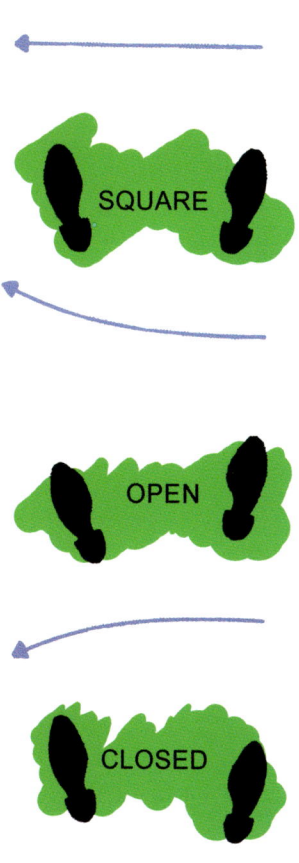

The Stance

Those of you who establish a certain pattern in taking your stance over the ball, will find it easier to feel confident and sure of your game as well as making the proper address position every time.
When you've decided on your stance, stand directly opposite the ball with both feet closed together. The ball should be more or less on a line with your feet. Now move your left foot toward the target and then finally your right foot into its position (Set-up in diagram is for the driver).

A correct stance on your full shots has the left toe turned out about 45% and the right foot almost perpendicular to the line of flight. Positioned this way, you're less likely to sway away from the target on the backswing. The right foot acts as a preventative counter balance. When the left foot is turned out, a path is prepared for the down and through part of the swing. The left hip must be cleared or pivoted out of the way during the downswing. If it is not, the hands will be impeded and a weaker shot will prevail. The shot will probably be off to the right as well.

The Stance

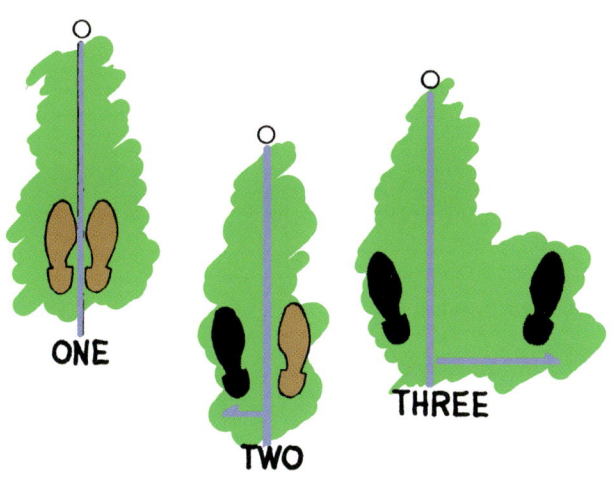

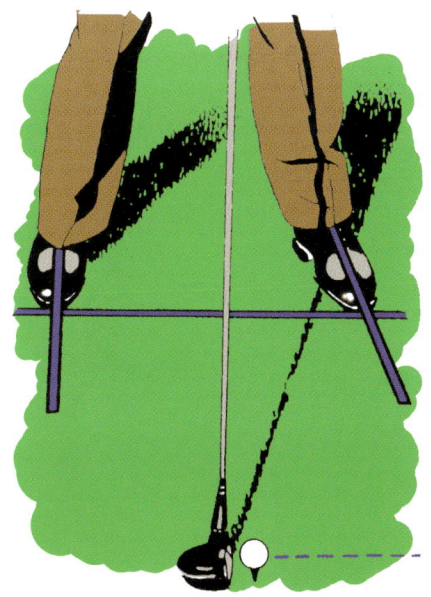

Billy Casper's Golf Tips

The Stance

In a way, golf is a knock-kneed game. It is definitely better to keep your weight inside your body at all times rather than letting it drift to the outside. If you allow this to happen you will probably sway off target or lose your balance or both.

Start out at address with both knees flexed slightly inward. At this point, the right knee should be in a little more than the left. The inward right knee will help prevent a sway during the backswing. The inward left knee helps keep the weight from moving to the outside of the left foot during the downswing and impact.

Teeing Tips

For drives, tee the ball so that half of it appears to be above the clubface when it is at the address position.
You are then able to impact the ball at the clubface centre, when the club is properly past the lowest point of its downward arc. This will naturally lift the ball into a correct trajectory for distance and better accuracy.

TEEING TIPS

If you tee the ball lower, you might find your backswing too steep as you are trying to lift the ball up. This will cause a major hook or slice. Teed too high and the clubhead can sweep through the ball and pop it nicely into the air, cutting your distance dramatically.

THE SWING

The Swing

As I have mentioned before, swings differ according to the player. To be effective, they must be compact, with all the moving parts working together.

On the full swing, the clubhead is brought back until the shaft is behind the back and horizontal to the ground. For some players this can be so exaggerated that the club is pointed back towards the ground. With a three-quarter swing, the club shaft is at about a 45% angle while a short or half swing is literally pointed straight up in the air.

The fullness of the swing does not necessarily affect the distance of your shot. The point to remember is to use a swing that is comfortable and suited to you. Don't let it get away from you or become uncontrollable. If you use the correct fundamentals of the grip, stance and swing there is a much better chance of hitting the shot you want. Whether you have an upright swing or a flat one is your personal choice and should make you comfortable.

The long irons and especially the woods are particularly hard to master. Built for distance, the woods have the longest shafts with an almost upright face and a flat bottom. There is no leading edge to bite the grass with making it the most feared club in an amateurs hands. A good point to remember when mastering the woods is to never attempt to pour more power into the shot. You will lose distance and accuracy. The key is a nice easy swing that takes into account the entire body. The backswing is key and should be slow and smooth. Once brought back as far as it can go, pause ever so slightly and then allow the recoil to bring the club back down and through. First the hips help to start the recoil and then the shoulders, arms and hands unleash like a giant spring.

The Swing

I have always felt that you should not put too much emphasis on the weight shifting. I think this is natural and as the club is brought back, the natural tendency is to throw the weight onto the right foot. As you bring the club down and through, the weight naturally shifts to the left foot.

As I've said, there are many things that go through golfers' minds when on the tee or over a shot. How much can a golfer possibly remember all at once? In attempting to heed all the advice a player's been given, he can get so confused he loses concentration altogether and misses the shot or hits it wildly.

I personally try to check myself on the backswing. I have a tendency to get too quick. Generally, I think about where I want the ball to go to give me my best next shot but occasionally I speed up too much. For the average golfer, the main points to remember are to keep your head down and still, keep the wrists stiff and follow through with the swing. The shift of the body weight and the co-ordination of hands, arms, shoulders and hips will become second nature.

The Swing

Backswing

In the address position the back of the left hand faces the target and moves directly at the target at and after impact. This assures accuracy, since the left hand controls the direction of the clubface. My hands are working well together when I can achieve this position. After impact, I swing the back of the hand towards the target for as long as possible. Of course, the actual shot is made with both hands on the club.

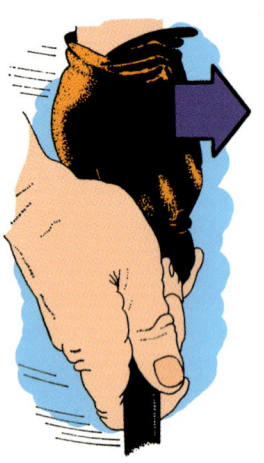

For most golfers, the left hand should be about a hands distance from the left leg at address. This position is for a driver and with shorter irons this distance decreases. The only way to check this is to have a friend take a look at your address position. If your left hand is farther away, you may tip forward onto your toes. If it is closer, you'll probably rock back on your heels.

The position of the right elbow at address is important too. The outside of the right elbow should face away from the golfer at an angle away from the target. The right arm should be free of tension with the elbow bent and almost touching your body. Positioned this way the right arm will bend or fold easily during the backswing. The right arm will stay comfortably close to the body. This can greatly minimise a sliced shot.

The Swing

Waggling the clubhead a few times over the ball helps you get used to the motion of the swing. You don't want to hit a ball from a dead start, which is what you would be doing if you neglect the waggle. Cultivate a smooth, swinging waggle until you use the procedure before every swing. Doing this will help your hands and fingers get used to the idea of holding the club while it is in motion.

I personally use only two waggles, and then I get my swing into motion without much delay. You may need more or less, but stick to the same procedure every time for added consistency and confidence.

The Swing

Imagination has a lot to do with the golf swing. Imagining how the clubface should be at impact will actually lead to a subconscious movement of your body muscles to that position.

One of the greatest distance killers in the golf swing is the sway away from the target during the backswing. When this happens the swing is robbed of the necessary centrifugal action required for a good distance shot.

If you are not getting the distance you want or think you should, check to see if your right leg is moving on your backswing. Here's a tip to help. Get a stick and place it in the ground just outside your right foot. If your knee hits it when you swing, you're swaying. Continue practising with the stick until you no longer come in contact with your right leg and you will cure your distance problem.

As the backswing begins, with the left arm and shoulder under control, the wrists remain as they were at address, straight, until they begin to cock at about halfway up the backswing. This helps to keep the clubface square to the intended target at the most important part of the swing.

You should feel a good extension of your left side muscles as you swing the clubhead back. To promote this extension, always start the clubhead back as low as possible to the ground. This will lead to a wider backswing arc. The best way to do this is to feel you are more or less pushing the clubface back with you left hand. Your right hand and arm are passive at this point.

If the backswing arc isn't wide enough or is cramped you won't build up any upper body coiling power for the impact. Begin your backswing with your left hand, arm and shoulder and move the clubhead back low to the ground. Do not use your wrists until you're past the halfway point in your backswing. If you feel your left side stretching, odds are you're swinging correctly.

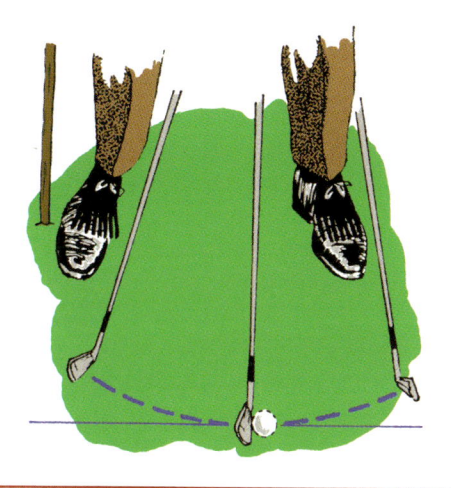

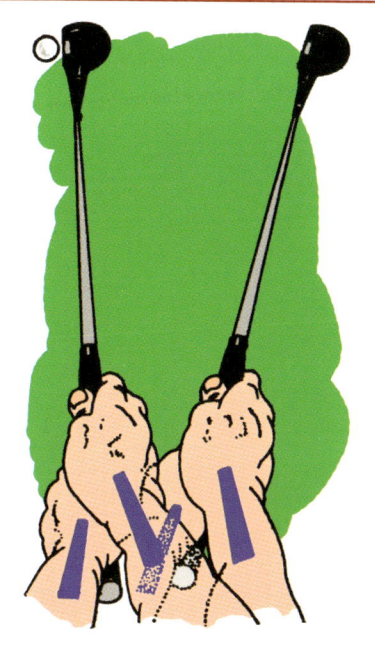

The Swing

Billy Casper's Golf Tips

The Swing

The left wrist and the back of the left forearm should form an essentially straight line at the top of the backswing. When you can do this, you have gone a long way toward keeping the clubface square to the intended target; that is, if the club is swung so that the shaft is horizontal to the ground at the top of the swing. All swings don't need to be that long, but the left wrist and forearm should always be straight at the top.

At the top of the backswing, the shaft should be pointing directly at the intended target. If the shaft is pointing to the right of the target, you have swung back too far inside and you will probably hit the ball to the left or hook it.

If the shaft points to the left, you'll slice the ball to the right because you are swinging from the outside in.

The Swing

Downswing

By using their hands and wrists too early, many golfers lose clubhead speed as they start the downswing. This usually produces a weak swing in which the clubhead approaches the ball from outside the intended line, and then cuts across and causes a slice.

If you move as slowly as possible as you start the downswing and think about beginning your motion with your body and not your hands, you will retain the wrist cock achieved at the top of the backswing.

The first downswing move should be a lateral slide of the hips towards the target. This places the weight properly on the left side and will eventually lead to solid contact with the ball.

The Swing

Throughout the downswing, the straight left arm keeps the clubhead in a constant arc. This gives you your best chance for a solid, square hit. If you extend your left arm at address and keep it straight as you swing back and down, you will be able to get the clubhead squarely onto the ball without too much trouble.

In order to realise your own power potential, get your right side into the shot during the downswing. As you move into the impact area, you should feel as if you are pushing off with your right foot, specifically your right toes. If you are going to make a free move through the ball, your right heel has to come up slightly.

At the same time, your right knee moves towards the target. At impact, it should be pointed directly at your ball.

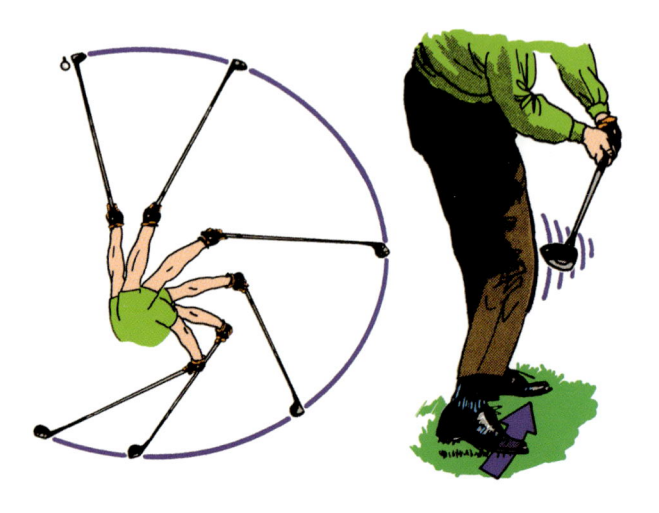

The Swing

I believe the most effective way of keeping the swing arc properly inside the target line is to move the right elbow in tight to the body on the downswing.

There is no restriction on the right elbow movement away from the body on the backswing, but once you start your downswing, move that elbow in close. If it stays there right through the impact with the ball, you'll get a square hit.

Just before impact, the wrists unlock and the clubhead is released into the ball. To help you maintain your wrist cock before impact, start your downswing as slow as possible and aim the butt of the club (top grip) at your ball. This will help to keep the wrists cocked until the proper moment to release.

Billy Casper's Golf Tips

The Swing

Accuracy is achieved by keeping the clubface absolutely square to the swing arc throughout the entire action. When this is done, the face is also square at impact.

At impact, the hands must be ahead of the clubhead. This is the position that puts power into the shot as it enables the hands to slam through the ball with force. If the hands are lagging behind the clubhead at impact, a weak uppercut hit is the result.

At impact, the best shots come from having a very firm left side. The left wrist, especially, should not be allowed to collapse. When this happens, the clubhead passes the hands in a little flipping motion that will kill the power of your shot. Allow the left hand and wrist to lead the clubhead through and past the ball's original position. The back of the left hand should move towards the target.

An indication of a properly active right side is the position of the right knee. As you drive into the ball, the right knee should flex inwards toward the target. When this happens, your body falls into a good hitting position, as long as your left side holds firm.

As you begin the downswing, move your weight quickly to your left side. Swing your right shoulder down and under past your chin. These actions will help you keep your upper body properly behind the ball on impact. You will get that accelerated whip into the ball, which won't happen if your head and shoulders move past the ball.

The Swing

Billy Casper's Golf Tips

The Swing

If you are raising up or somehow altering the path of the clubhead through impact and not getting the power you want or even a solid hit, this tip might help you.

After every iron shot from a normal lie, simply watch for the divot to appear before you allow your head and eyes to raise and follow the ball. If you think through this, your subconscious will help to keep your head and eyes down and this will result in a better more solid shot.

Every golfer has heard that he must keep his head down in order to make good contact with the ball. This is essentially true, but there is a danger in becoming too rigid and messing up your neck muscles. Be sure to keep loose and let your head naturally come up when your arms are at least shoulder height on your follow through after impact.

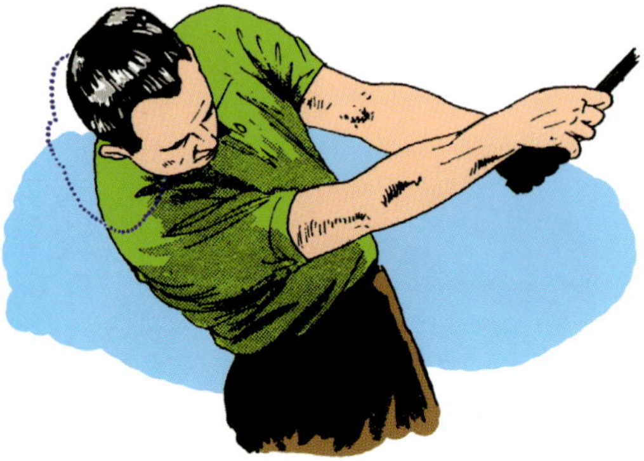

FAIRWAY SHOTS

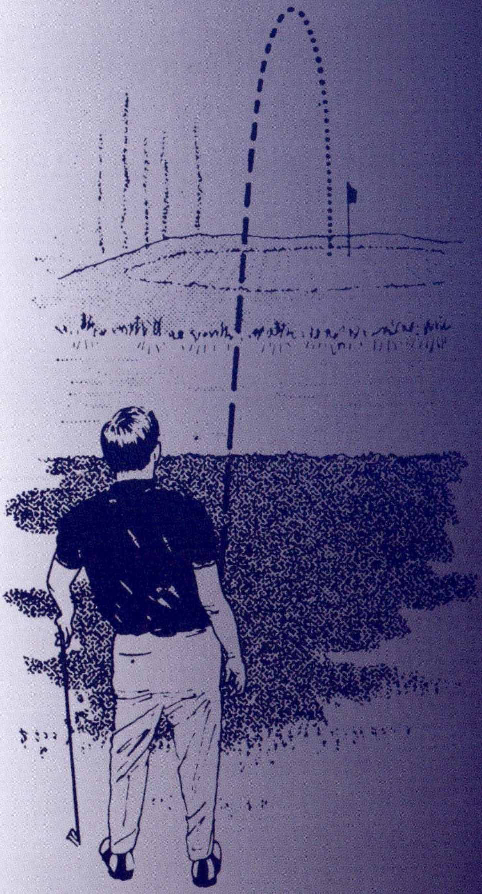

Fairway Shots

Many average golfers are uncomfortable using their woods. These comprise the Driver or 1 wood, 3 wood, 4 wood, 5 wood or 7 wood. I would first say that you need to become comfortable with your woods on the tee and then on the fairways. Because of the longer shaft and the almost straight up and down face, you are able to get a longer swing arc and more power in the shot. The woods help to give you the distance you need on today's long golf courses and it is worth spending the extra half hour on the range working on them.

The irons can be broken down into three categories. The 2,3 and 4 irons are considered long irons for distances ranging from 240 down to 160 yards. The middle irons are the 5,6 and 7 and go roughly 170 yards down to 130 yards. The short irons, which consist of the 8, 9, and the wedges, go from 140 yards down to 30 yards depending upon individual style and power.

Distance really is immaterial and you should concentrate on your own game and your own power. Average golfers, much the same as touring professionals, sometimes try to squeeze more power out of the shot when the shot would be better executed and closer to the target if you took one more club and swung 10% easier. I normally swing with about 80% of my full power. It is possible for me to hit a 7 iron 175 yards but it would be self defeating, as I would have to use my full power. I would be smarter to pick up a 6 iron and swing easier.

Fairway Shots

Average golfers tend to look at yardage charts and other information they see in magazines and golf related articles. Unfortunately, most of these are geared to the above average golfer or touring professional and it can get confusing finding your own distances. In my opinion, one of the best skills you can learn on the golf course is your own yardages. Make up your own chart either written or in memory. If you know the distance you hit a 7 iron or 5 iron then you are a step ahead when you come up to your ball. It takes a lot of the guesswork out of the game and undoubtedly will make it more enjoyable and easier to score.

Fairway Shots

Knowing how far you can hit your irons is one of the best ways to build confidence on the course. If you know your game and your distance then you can hit better shots, simply because you are more comfortable over the ball. The place to figure out your personal distances is at the driving range. Have definite targets you are hitting to and take a notepad along if you feel you can't memorise it all.

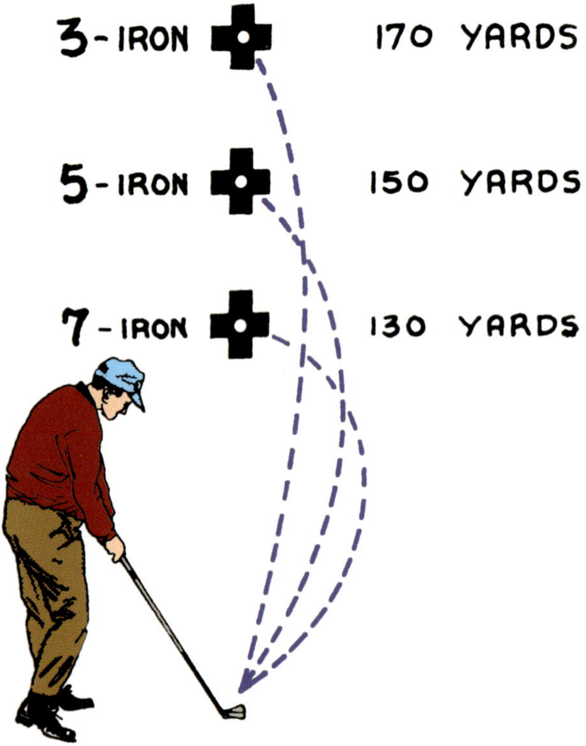

3-IRON — 170 YARDS

5-IRON — 150 YARDS

7-IRON — 130 YARDS

Fairway Shots

You can use the following chart as a rough guide but as I've said, these distances are usually achieved by a middle to low handicapper. Don't get frustrated if you're not there yet!

Club	Distance
2-iron	210-230 yards
3-iron	200-220 yards
4-iron	190-210 yards
5-iron	180-200 yards
6-iron	170-190 yards
7-iron	160-180 yards
8-iron	150-170 yards
9-iron	140-160 yards
P-wedge	110-150 yards
S-wedge	50 -110 yards
L-wedge	30 – 80 yards

Remember the basics we have already discussed; grip, stance and swing. Your grip remains the same with all the clubs, except perhaps the putter. Your stance, however, changes depending on the length of the iron or wood. A long iron or wood has a long shaft and therefore, for balance and control, the stance should be approximately shoulder width or slightly wider. The shorter irons demand a slightly narrower stance with the left foot withdrawn a bit. This takes some of the left side out of the shorter shots and gets the ball into the air better.

My cardinal rule is to always swing easy, swing well within your self and learn your own game to score better!

Fairway Shots

You should assess every shot from behind the ball before you assume your stance. Sometimes the target looks different at address than from behind the ball and looking behind the ball will give you a better view and layout of the hole.

As you walk up to the ball, get it between you and the target. Pause a moment to imagine just how you want to hit the shot and where you want it to fly. Start to create a mental picture of the club you are going to use and the style of shot you want to play. Once this is decided, you'll be ready for a good swing as you step up to the ball and you won't have to think over those aspects while in your address position.

Fairway Shots

For long shots in light to medium rough, many golfers will automatically reach for an iron. This is alright but don't sacrifice needed distance when you don't have to. A 4 or 5 wood can cut through quite a bit of grass. It's heavier, so you don't have to swing as hard and the longer shaft produces a wider swing arc putting more power into the shot.

Play the ball off the left heel and open the clubface and stance a bit. Stand a little closer to the ball than usual so you produce a much more upright swing arc and break your wrists a little more than usual on the backswing. This will help you to swing directly down on the ball and you'll be able to get it out of the rough nicely.

Fairway Shots

Long irons (2, 3 and 4) are especially helpful on holes where you need good length and accuracy. Properly hit, a long iron shot will give you the distance close to one of your woods but with the ability to stop in a relatively short distance on the green. If hit properly, you can get good backspin with a long iron, and you just can't get that with a wood.

The long iron swing is more of a sweep than an abrupt hit. Keep this in mind when you hit this shot. Sometimes the difficulty with a long iron stems from the ball position. Don't let yourself get cramped in your sweeping long iron swing. Move the ball forward in your stance. This gives you room to take a good full-bodied swing at the ball. Another good point is to position your hands over the ball at address, not behind it. You want to get as much loft into the clubface to get the ball airborne.

Fairway Shots

Billy Casper's Golf Tips

Fairway Shots

Many golfers hook or slice their long irons because they have the clubface out of position at the address. To be truly online to your target see that the bottom line of the clubface is exactly lined up to the target. If your clubface is not square at the address, you will never be able to get it back in the proper position before you strike the ball.

INCORRECT

CORRECT

Fairway Shots

The only time this is not applicable are for those times when you need to hit a "trick" shot to get out of trouble. These are called a draw or hook and a fade or slice.

To hook the ball, it is necessary to put a counter-clockwise spin on it. You do this by swinging inside you normal line and closing the face of the club slightly. Use a closed stance, with the right foot withdrawn more than the left.

To slice the ball, it is necessary to put a clockwise spin on it. You do this by swinging outside your normal line and opening up the face of the club slightly. Use an open stance, with your left foot withdrawn more than the right.

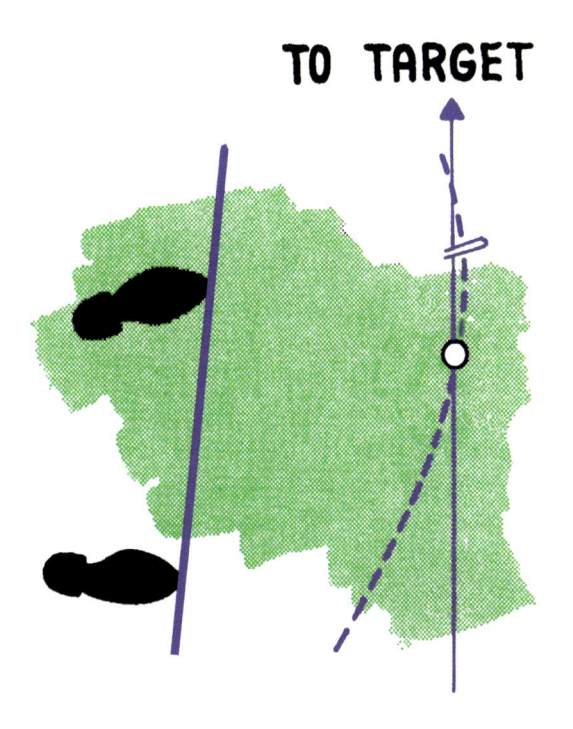

TO TARGET

Fairway Shots

When the ball is above your feet, control becomes extremely important. If you hold the club as you normally do, you will be too far away for a good swing at the ball. is best to choke down on the grip. The more severe the slope, the more you should choke the club.

Always set yourself up to the right of the target for the ball tends to hook or pull from this kind of lie. Your knees don't need as much flex because you are trying to stand tall but keep them relaxed. With a shortened grip, it is also a good idea to limit your backswing. I always try to swing my left hand at the target. This works well and helps the body get into position on these types of shots.

Downhill lies create a problem all of their own. It is very difficult to stay down on the shot from this sort of lie and get the ball in the air.

Think of this and try to compensate with your swing.

A couple of other things that are important are, remember to aim left. The ball has a natural tendency to fly to the right on these shots. Play the ball in the centre of your stance or even back of centre. At address, level your hips by bending more at your right knee than at the left and use a club you are confident about getting the ball in the air with.

Above all else, stay down and try to move the clubhead along the ground for as long as you can after impact.

Fairway Shots

Billy Casper's Golf Tips

Fairway Shots

To add loft to your shot, you need to play the ball more forward in your stance than usual. Keep your hands behind the ball and open up the clubface, so that it faces to the right of your intended target line. The ball will probably fade a little bit, so keep this in mind when you are lining up.

Swing the clubhead back low and then as upright as possible. You want to sweep the ball up. Imagining this shot before you hit it will make a big difference too.

Fairway Shots

When a proper downward swing is made with any iron, the clubhead should take a divot in front of the ball's original position. The idea is to strike the ball first then moving downward for a bit past the ball and taking the divot at this time.

With this kind of impact, the clubhead squeezes the ball against the turf, giving maximum backspin and producing the straightest shots. When you take a divot, you will get a surprise with the distance as well. You get better impact and control but also greater distance when you use this sequence and take a nice divot.

Fairway Shots

When the ball is resting close to the ground with a tight or sparse lie, there is no need to alter the swing much. If it makes you feel more confident, play the ball more in the center of your stance. This will put your hands a little more ahead of the ball. If you do this too much, however, you will lose height on the shot and lose distance. Stay down on the shot during and after impact.

Fairway Shots

With shorter irons you are always better off choking down an inch or so on the grip. You may also want to use a slightly stronger iron and play the ball more inside your left foot than usual. Bring the clubface powerfully into the shot, almost pinching the ball against the ground. You will hit a better shot and find that you have taken a divot that is directly in line with your target.

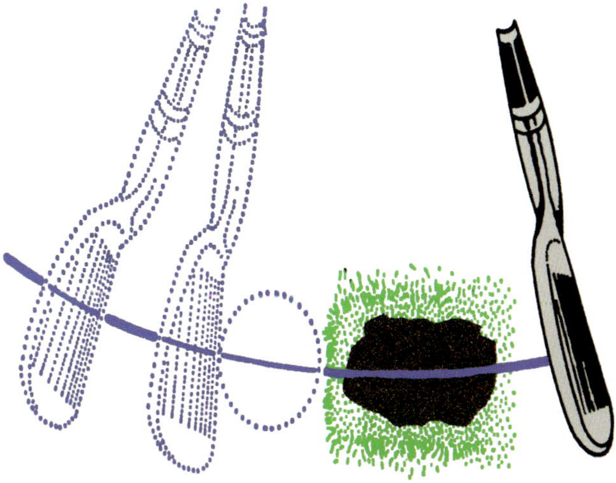

Fairway Shots

From all but the lightest rough, the clubface should be opened more than the woods. When the club must travel through any kind of grass, the face will nearly always close a bit on impact. This is because the grass grabs at the hosel and slows it down considerably, bringing the clubface around.

If you start with an open face it will counteract this and will help to achieve a higher, straighter shot from any kind of rough.

On longer shots, from your driver to the long irons, backspin helps and steadies the ball during flight. When you hit shorter shots, it is what helps the ball stop on the green, preferably close to the hole!

To get good backspin, you need to weld the ball against the clubface at impact. On a good shot, the ball will be struck at the point just below the vertical center of the clubface, then it will climb up a little bit as the swing continues. This is what starts it backspinning. Another helpful reminder is to play the ball slightly further back in your stance allowing your hands at impact to be slightly ahead of the ball.

Billy Casper's Golf Tips

Fairway Shots

The high, soft shot over a bunker or water to the green is one you face often on today's golf courses.

Using a short iron or wedge, position your hands behind the ball at address. The ball is played forward off the left foot in a slightly open stance. This position helps the loft of the clubface.

Move your hands a quarter turn to the left so that your wrists don't turn over at impact. Swing with the feeling that you are slipping the clubface directly under the ball, without turning you wrists. You should take a nice divot in front of the original ball position.

Fairway Shots

Knowing where to aim on every shot is important and can overcome some swing deficiencies.

A good rule of thumb is to plan every shot so that your next shot is easier. Aim for a place on the fairway that will give you the safest approach shot to the green.

On the illustrated hole, the 517 yard par 5 1st at the Dukes Golf Club in St. Andrews, Scotland, you would want to hit the ball in the middle of the fairway, taking out of play the bunkers on the right and the wild rough on the left.

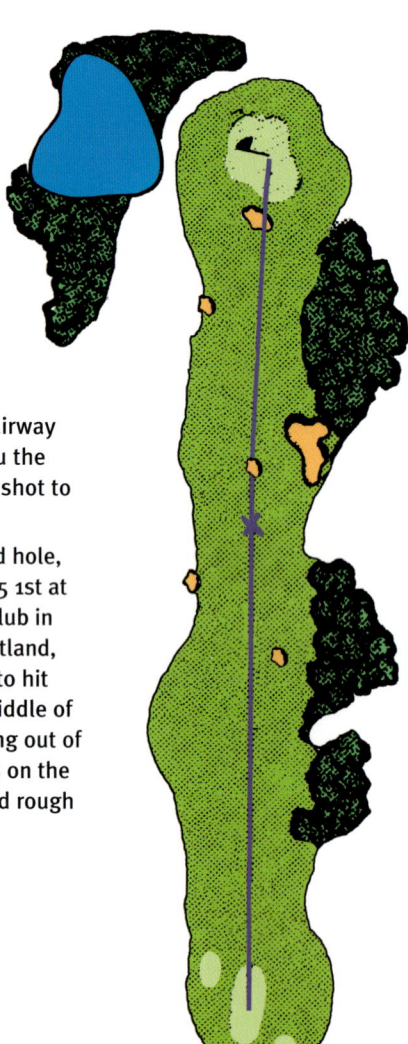

AROUND THE GREEN

Around the Green

I am a big believer in the chip and run shot when the ball is just off the green. I like to get the ball on the green fast and with the least amount of trouble from the fringe as possible. Because of the quality of courses these days, especially the greens, compared with years ago, a lot of pros prefer to putt from off the green. Others prefer to punch the ball towards the hole giving it more loft and then biting into the green.

The chip and run shot is a product of British courses, where traditionally the fringe is tough and wiry and the greens hard from the winds and weather. Putting from off the green (or Texas wedge if you prefer) was developed in the southwest of America, where the fringes and greens are hard and tightly manicured.

When I am hitting a chip and run shot, I will generally use a 5, 6 or 7 iron. These all have a minimum amount of loft. I first study the terrain and the roll of the green and then I pick a spot where I want the ball to land, figuring approximately how much roll is needed to get the ball to the hole.

For the average once a week golfer, I would suggest spending 15 minutes practising chip shots before each round. Pick out tough lies and other obstacles and then practice getting the ball close to the hole. This pre-round practice will build your confidence and help you to have better feel around the greens.

Around the Green

The object of being just off the green is to get down in two. This means getting the ball close enough to the hole to need only one putt to finish.

In today's modern golf, putting is probably the most important aspect for pros. Today's players have a brute strength we didn't have in my early days on the tour and being repetitious machines when it comes to iron and wood play makes putting the name of the game. I personally think that all facets are important but tournaments are won or lost on and around the greens. The next time you read about or watch a professional event, note how many birdie putts the winner made throughout his four rounds.

Around the Green

I use a chip and run shot when shooting to a hard green that generally won't hold a medium iron shot. This would also be true if you had the wind behind you or you are trying to keep the ball low because of a tree or other impediments.

To hit this shot, you need to play the ball towards your right foot. This will put your hands ahead of the ball and it lessens the effective loft of the clubface. Be sure the clubface is pointed at the target. Swing back as low as possible and do not use too much backswing. Try to come into the ball low with your hands ahead of the clubhead. Also try to keep the clubhead square to the target as long as possible after contact.

Around the Green

I like to chip primarily using my arms and shoulders, although I do move my body a little bit to keep a fluid motion.

For a normal chip, the stance should be narrow and slightly open. I also move my left foot back slightly, giving me more room for my shoulders to swing. The ball should be played in the center of the stance and the clubhead should be square at impact. This way the ball can readily roll in a straight line when it lands.

Around the Green

Whenever it is possible, try to hit your chip so that it rolls the last 2/3 of the distance to the hole.

To do this, use a club with the least amount of loft that will get the ball on the green. Ideally, the closer you are to the green, the less loft you should use.

Pick a spot on the green where you want the ball to land and then before you hit the shot imagine how hard you are going to hit it to get it there. Swing the club back low and without too much wrist break. Then accelerate into the ball.

Before you hit every chip shot you should try and plan how you want your shot to go. Once you do this, you will find it that much easier to execute a good golf shot.

Good chippers keep a simple rule in mind. Use a lower loft club the closer you are to the green. A low shot is always preferred, because it will run better onto the greeen with much less chance of a bad sideways bounce. Also, don't make your target too small, or you may become nervous about getting it close. Try and picture a circle approximately 1-3 feet in diameter around the hole. You will be amazed at how much more confidence you have trying to get the ball into that area.

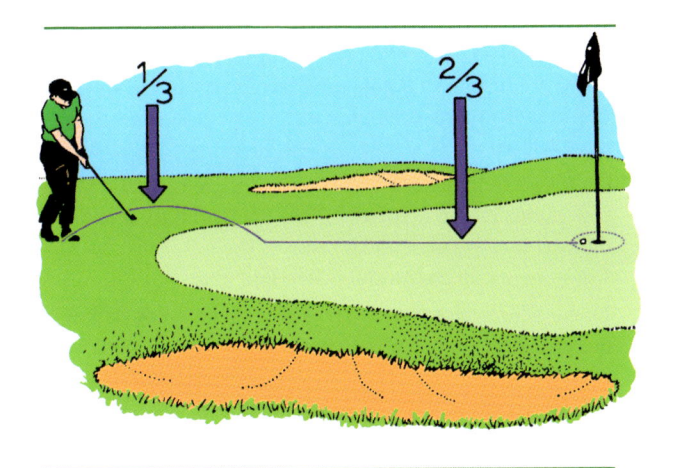

Around the Green

Billy Casper's Golf Tips

Around the Green

You can always expect a low shot from a hard or bare lie. If you are hitting to a green, plan to hit a run up shot. The idea is to land the ball short of the green and then let it run on.

Play the ball in the center of your stance and position your hands ahead of the ball. This hoods the clubface, tilting it forward a bit and it reduces the loft. I always shorten my grip on the club when I do this.

Take a shorter than usual backswing and clip the ball off the ground taking very little divot. Also strike the ball first, because if you hit the ground before you hit the ball the club will bounce and you will skull the ball.

Around the Green

The full backspin shot can be hit best from firm turf and short grass. It is also best hit from no more than 100–120 yards. Use a narrow and square stance. Play the ball in the back half of your stance and slightly towards your right foot. Also, keep your weight to the left as you swing and come down hard and abruptly onto the ball. This sharp downward stroke will give you maximum backspin on the shot.

Around the Green

Never play the ball too far back in your stance for an ordinary fairway shot.
You don't want your hands to get too far forward in front of the ball or you will hit a low shot.

The proper wedge position is to play the ball perhaps two inches inside the left heel, with your hands very slightly ahead of the ball. You can open your stance, but not too much. Your turned out left foot should have the toe about an inch or so below of the right foot.

Around the Green

Shooting out of the Sand

Foot and body position is very important on all golf shots including those from the sand. If you have this in place, it makes it much easier to execute a good swing.

From normal sand (not packed or hard sand) the idea is to swing the clubhead through the sand underneath the ball. The clubhead should not touch the ball because the force of the club going through the sand will pop the ball up. The arc of the swing should be a very wide flattened "U" shape.

Play the ball off the left heel with a very open and narrow stance, hands slightly behind the ball. Plan to strike the sand with the face of the club looking at the pin. You should also target an area around two inches behind the ball to strike the sand. The face of the club should not turn over at impact so you need to hold tightly with the left hand. Don't stop at impact. Make sure you follow through completely.

Billy Casper's Golf Tips

Around the Green

One of the most troublesome shots is from a buried lie in the sand. In order to get the ball out and flying towards the green you must swing so that your sandwedge digs deeply into the sand from a point close to the ball.

When you address the ball, turn the face of the club or close it so that it looks towards the target. Keep your hands well in front of the ball and swing steep.

The backswing and downswing are both much steeper in order to punch through the sand. Break your wrists early; as you go into your backswing then swing directly down at a spot no more than one inch behind the ball. Your grip must be firm and don't leave the clubhead in the sand. You must follow through.

Around the Green

If you know where to aim in the sand then it is much easier to get the ball out of it.

For a level lie, you want to hit the sand about 1 1/2 – 2 inches behind the ball.

For an uphill lie, you want to hit the sand less than 1 inch behind the ball. If the lie is extreme, try to hit the ball and sand at the same time.

For a downhill lie, you want to hit the ball more than 2 inches behind the ball. The down swing should be abrupt and very steep.

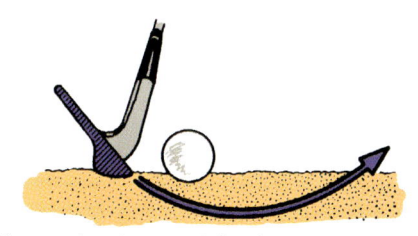

Normal - 1 1/2 - 2 inches

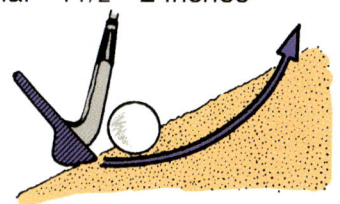

Uphill - less than 1 inch

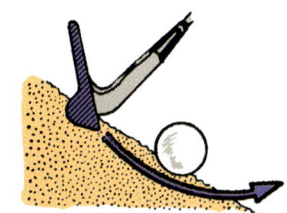

Downhill - 2 inches or more

Around the Green

When hitting out of the sand, the idea is to take a slice of sand out from under the ball. Ideally, the clubhead should never really hit the ball. The exceptions being when you have an extreme uphill lie or the sand is hard packed (wet). In these circumstances try to hit the ball and the sand at the same time, sliding the club under the ball.

Take an extremely open stance (left foot withdrawn much more than the right) over the ball and position your hands behind the ball. You are more likely to hit the sand a couple of inches behind the ball by doing this. Also, weaken your grip by placing your left hand to the side and your right hand more on top than usual.

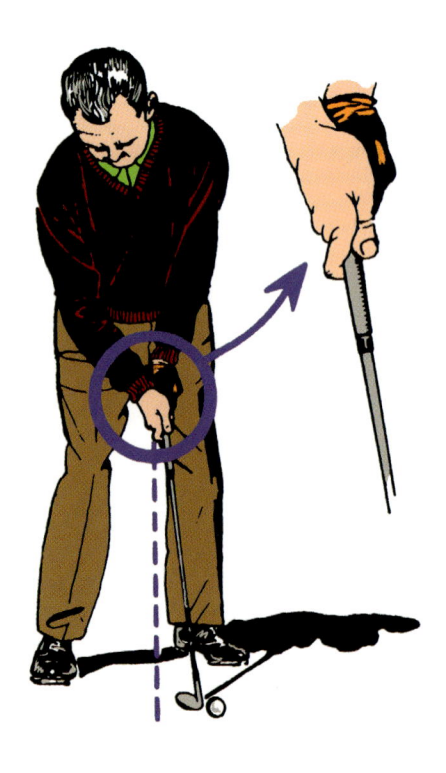

ON THE GREEN

On the Green

To people who follow golf, the successes I have had in my career are generally attributed to my putting and short game. Some have said that if you had taken the putter out of my hand, then I would have been just another golfer. I am still amazed that this legend lives on. In my opinion there are better putters on tour than I have been and I personally feel that my game from tee to green is as good if not better than my short game. I do, however, remember how this all got started.

In 1959, I was playing in the US Open Championship at Winged Foot Golf Club in New York. At this point in my career, few Easterners and even fewer people overseas knew anything about me. The favorites were Ben Hogan, Sam Snead and a young newcomer named Arnold Palmer, who had won the previous year's Masters tournament.

On the first day of the tournament I shot a 71 and only used 28 putts. The next day I shot 68 with 30 putts and lead the event by one shot over Ben Hogan and Arnold Palmer. Nobody was greatly impressed and the media classed me as some jolly fat man. Admittedly, I did weigh 220 pounds at this stage, but I would never have considered myself jolly. I always thought that Ben Hogan had the right idea on the golf course: the golf course is the equivalent of our office and you take business seriously at the "office".

People started taking me more seriously when I used only 27 putts in the third round and managed to shoot a 69 on a rain soaked day. This gave me a 3-stroke lead going into the final day. During the final round I was stung by a bee and suffered greatly on the course but managed to hold on for the win with a 282. It was recorded that I had 114 putts for the four rounds and from then on the label stuck: Billy Casper: The Putter.

On the Green

50 percent of golfers' strokes are on or around the green. I think the ideal way to teach golf from the beginning is to start with the putting and then work your way up. This is the reverse of how most people learn golf, but I don't think people spend enough time on their short games.

Greater attention should be given to chipping and putting because you will spend a lot of your time around the greens. Believe it or not, you can hook a putt or a chip shot as easily as you can hook a drive.

Not everyone has Jack Nicklaus' or Tiger Woods' strength but everyone can learn to chip and putt accurately.

On the Green

Putting is an individual art. There is no right way or formula that will make you into a great putter but there are some important basics that will help keep you on the right track. First, you must always keep the putter face square to the target. Also, use an unhurried stroke but make solid contact with the ball. Finally, try to keep your shoulders moving along a straight line towards the target.

I never recommend that anyone copy my particular style of putting. You must adopt a stance and grip that makes you comfortable over the ball. One of the keys to good consistent putting is comfort and confidence. There are many putters to choose from. Find one that fits you like a glove and that you have confidence in, then practice the preparation of the putt. In other words, learn how to read greens, understand the grain in the grass and the undulations on the green. I know some good putters who even put themselves into a kind of trance and visualise the ball dropping into the hole. Practising whatever works for you will give you the confidence to be a good putter and will help you score better.

A good point to remember is that a stroke saved around the green counts the same as one lost because of a bad drive or wayward iron shot.

On the Green

If there is one universal fundamental in putting it is the immovable head. Those who keep their heads steady are usually good on the green.

This doesn't mean you should concentrate so hard you tighten your muscles. This would make your body too tense and would interfere with a nice smooth stroke. If you can keep your head down over the ball until it is half way to the cup, it will do wonders for your putting. The steady head helps the body to avoid swaying, resulting in a mis-hit.

On the Green

Most putts are missed because of a half-hearted stroke at the ball. Every putt should be made with firm hands, solid impact and enough speed to get to the hole on the intended line. The clubhead should move past the ball's original position after impact.

I like to think that I am holding the clubface in position with my left hand and hitting it with my right. Don't let the left hand turn in any direction and make sure you accelerate through the ball towards the hole.

If you go onto the green with a heavy heart, thinking about the mistakes you made previously, you will rarely sink that needed putt. Good putters are equally as determined to get the ball into the hole as they are to forgive and forget the past mistakes and get on with trying to score.

Hesitation can be a killer on the green too. Have you picked the right line? Are your hands and shoulders in line? If you have doubts, chances are you will slow down your putting stroke and the ball will easily go off line. Once you choose the line of the putt and how hard you have to hit it, step up and putt, keeping in mind the acceleration through the ball. This is important on all putts, but especially the short knee knockers.

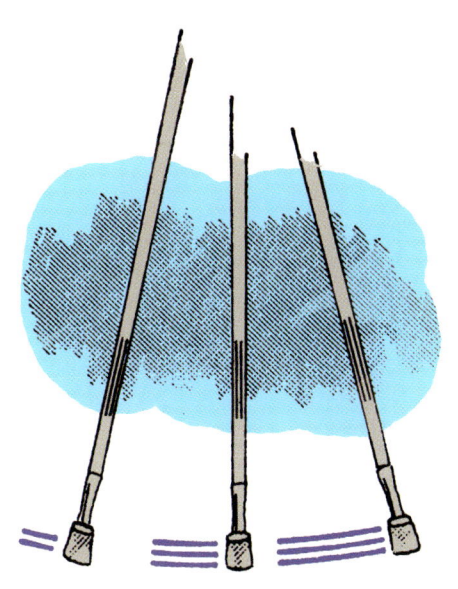

On the Green

Billy Casper's Golf Tips

On the Green

Looking at the illustration, notice my shoulders and hips have not turned away from the line parallel to the line of the putt. In my particular style, I allow my wrists to break freely on the backswing. I don't turn or rotate my hands, which brings the clubface too far inside the intended line.

By far the most important part is that my upper body and my head have not moved away from the intended direction on the backswing and follow through.

On the Green

If you are missing most of your putts left, especially the longer ones, you are probably allowing the left wrist to break too soon at or after impact.

A good way of checking this is to stop yourself after impact and the follow through and hold that position. You should see the back of your left wrist pointing at the intended target. If you have allowed your wrist to break too early, the clubface will be closed on impact.

Use whatever wrist break is comfortable for you in the backswing but try to minimise it on the follow through for straighter, more accurate putts.

On the Green

A good way to get comfortable with your putting is to learn more about the read of the greens. Different grass on the greens makes a big difference in the strength of your putting as well as the break.

If the grass looks shiny from behind your ball, you can assume the grain is with you and the ball will run more easily along the intended line. If the grass is duller and dark then the grain is against you and you will have to hit the ball harder.

If you can't tell by looking from behind or in front of the ball than look at it from the side. Sometimes there are cross grains on the green and this has a tendency to hold a sidehill putt going uphill but gives a much more noticeable break in your putt if it is going downhill.

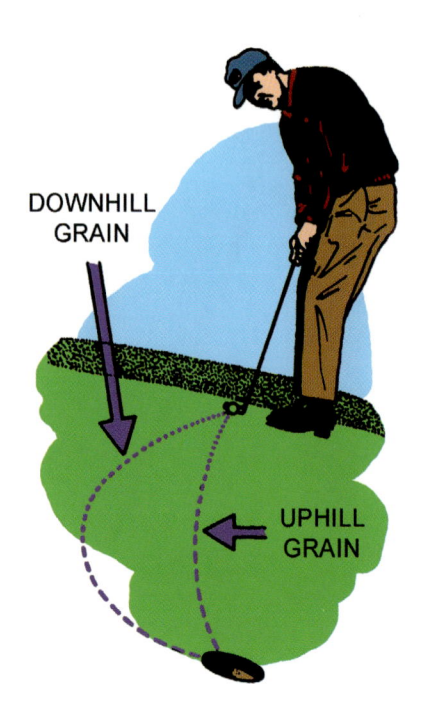

On the Green

As I have said, by far the most important part of putting is the steady head and you will be amazed at how many putts you will sink if this one problem is cured.

By keeping your head fixed and swinging along the intended line to the hole, you will become a better putter in no time with some dedicated practice.

If I had to sum up the one all important factor in the golf swing, on the putting green, fairway and the tee box it would be to keep your head down and follow through as much along the target line as possible.

This will give you more power, better feel, control, and an overall better golf game, not to mention being much more enjoyable too.

Two old fishing friends of mine, Sam Snead and Ted Williams (Boston Red Sox, baseball hero) debated for years about which is more difficult: hitting a golf ball or hitting a baseball coming towards you at 100 miles per hour. In response to Ted's certainty that it was much harder to hit a moving target, Sam replied, "Maybe so, but if you hit a foul ball in golf, you have to play it!"

With all there is to think about in the game of golf or more particularly your swing, it is important to enjoy it. At the end of the day, it is the enjoyment and thrill of hitting a golf ball exactly the way you wanted to that keeps us golfers, professional and amateur alike, coming back for more and more.

Interview with Billy Casper

I had a chance to spend some time with my Father at the Ryder Cup, Belfry 2002. We spoke endlessly about the new golf tips book and ways that we could make it more personable and interesting.

After the Ryder Cup, I decided to do an informal interview with Dad. This interview was done recently in San Diego, CA and Marrakech, Morocco.

Byron;
"I know you get asked this a lot, but it seems a good place to start. What would you say are your favorite ten courses in the world?"

Billy;
"There are some great golf course around the world but my personal favorites are. (Not necessarily in order);

1- Cypress Point, Monterey CA
2- San Diego CC, Chula Vista, CA
3- Royal Dar Es Salaam, Rabat, Morocco
4- Wingfoot GC, New York
5- Olympic GC, San Francisco, CA
6- Seminole GC, Palm Beach, FL
7- Colonial CC, Fort Worth, Tx
8- Medina GC, Chicago, IL
9- Muirfield GC, Gullane, Scotland
10- Augusta National GC, Augusta, GA"

"I am sure you must have great stories about all of these courses. Is there one in particular that brings up a special feeling or story more than most?"

"A few of the courses I have listed are favorites because of special wins and other memorable moments I had, but Augusta National, home of the Masters Golf Tournament, is close to my heart because the press used to say I would never win there; that it was set up wrong for my particular game and playing style. I eventually did win there in 1970 and it was a great feeling to prove all of them wrong!"

Interview with Billy Casper

"While we are talking about wins, which ones were the most memorable and why?"

"In addition to Augusta and my Masters win, there are also a few other wins that have a special place in my life, one of them being my very first win as a professional at the Labatt Open in Canada. The two US Open victories I have are very high on my list of favorite memories as well, and in 1963 after a major hand injury, where I didn't think I would ever swing a golf club again, I won the Insurance City Open and that was a great feeling. It gave me back the confidence in my game and in my health to go out and continue to play and win!"

"What would you say is your proudest moment as a professional golfer?"

"There have been a lot of times when I have been extremely grateful for what I have been able to achieve as a golfer and I am proud of so many things in my life but two of those moments that stand out are when I was inducted into the World Golf Hall of Fame in 1978 and then the PGA Hall of Fame in 1982"

"In your opinion, why was your putting the main focus of the media and press early on in your career?"

"In 1959 I was playing in the US Open. It was my 4th year on tour and earlier in the year I had failed to qualify at the Masters golf tournament. I knew a good performance at the Open was key to the rest of the year. Through out the four rounds I was putting well and scoring well and won the tournament but I remember I had only 114 putts for the tournament and after that the press seemed to give me the title, Billy Casper the putter!"

Interview with Billy Casper

Who are your biggest influences in golf? I guess what I mean is; who are your personal golfing heroes?"

"Ben Hogan is the first that comes to mind. He was a great man and a great golfer! I would have to say that the other two that I have are Byron Nelson and Sam Snead. Both great men and talented golfers."

Who are the other playing professionals whom you thought of as good competitors and great guys to be paired with?"

"Gay Brewer is one of my favorite people to play with and for years we have been partners in the Legends of Golf Tournament in Texas. My other favorites are Peter Aliss and Christy O'Connor."

"What do you consider to be one of the worst moments in your professional career?"

"There are a couple of times in my career that I have not been playing the way I wanted to but one of those times was in 1959. I had just missed the cut at the Masters and I wasn't sure if I was ever going to be eligible to play in it again. Later in the year I won the US Open and that gave me an exemption into the Masters tournament."

(I was caddying for my Dad at the time of this story) "What was the most expensive shot in your playing career?"

"When I was playing on the tour in my younger days, the money was a lot different from now. I remember my 1st US Open win in 1959; I received a check for 12,000 US dollars. You could add another zero to that and it would still be closer to second, third or fourth place in tournaments today. However, on the Senior PGA tour we played for some great prize money and

Interview with Billy Casper

one of those was an invitational in Tryall, Jamaica. First prize at this event was 500,000.00 US dollars. This tournament was open to the top ten Senior PGA players and the top ten LPGA players and this particular year I was paired with Jan Stephenson. On the final day we had caught up with the leaders and, coming down the 18th needed a birdie between us to win and par to go into a play off. We subsequently got into a play off and lost the first hole to two bad drives. I remember that the 2nd place prize money was something like 55,000.00 and thinking what a massive jump from first to second it was indeed."

"What helped you to focus on the golf course?"

"My commitment has always been towards taking the emotion out of my game. I have always tried to stay calm and cool under any pressure and my focus has purely been in concentration. Ben Hogan was one who had incredible concentration on the course and didn't get too excited one way or the other. This has been my style as well trying to meet every shot good or bad with an even keel and not get too bothered by it."

"What would you say the first and most important part of the game is? In other words, if you are teaching someone, what is the first thing you will look at and fix?"

"It would have to be the grip. First and foremost the grip is your only contact with the ball your body is going to have so it makes sense to get it right. I look at the grip and the size of hands the player has to decide which grip would suit their game best. Then you can work on the other fundamentals of stance and swing."

Interview with Billy Casper

"Who would you say gave you your start as a professional golfer and why?"

"After coming home from a semester at Notre Dame University in Indiana, I joined the US Navy. I spent most of my time at the naval training centre golf course and did a lot of teaching and playing. At the time I was playing in a lot of local San Diego competitions and it gained me the attention of a few people including two men who became my sponsors. I ended up with a three-year sponsor deal and in 1955 went off to play in my first event. The first tournament I played in was the Western Open in Portland, Oregon and I made my first ever pay check as a professional golfer. It was for 33 dollars and 33 cents."

"After playing around San Diego so much, who do you think had the most confidence in your ability to play professionally? The sponsors?"

"The sponsors did have faith in me and my playing ability but at the end of the day it was my wife, Shirley, and I who had the most confidence. We decided together that I should give it a shot and we haven't looked back since!

It's interesting to note that at the time, there were a lot of media people and even the famous San Diegan professional, Paul Runyan, who thought I would never make it as a professional, simply because they didn't think I was athletic enough and that my game wouldn't hold up to professional tournament golf!"

"With all that you have accomplished over the last 50 years, what are your plans for the future now?"

"I am going in for hip replacement surgery early in 2003 and then I plan to play in the Super Senior PGA Events. I am also still active in clinics and exhibitions as well as speaking appearances. On top of this, our

Interview with Billy Casper

golf course management group is now managing 42 golf clubs and I am very involved in golf course design with my partner, Greg Nash. My other interests lie in nutrition, publishing and fishing."

"Off the course you have always been a great speaker and I know you have a massive repertoire of golfing jokes and stories but how about closing this interview with one of your favorites?"

"Well... I like to say that it is important to swing hard... in case you hit it! And... don't be like the chronic golf cheater... he got a hole-in-one on a par three and marked 0 on the scorecard!"

Let me say that it was a unique privilege to interview my own Father. I had the opportunity to work with him closely on his new golf tips book.... "Billy Casper's Golf Tips" and now that I have had the opportunity to interview him, I have learned things about him I didn't even know!

I hope you have enjoyed the golf tips and also this small insight into my father, a legend in the golf world, a great family man and a person whom, in my opinion, we can all learn from.

Byron Casper